SWIMMING

by Claire Vanden Branden

Cody Koala
An Imprint of Pop!
popbooksonline.com

abdobooks.com

Published by Pop!, a division of ABDO, PO Box 398166, Minneapolis, Minnesota 55439. Copyright © 2020 by POP, LLC. International copyrights reserved in all countries. No part of this book may be reproduced in any form without written permission from the publisher. Pop!™ is a trademark and logo of POP, LLC.

Printed in the United States of America, North Mankato, Minnesota

102019
012020

THIS BOOK CONTAINS RECYCLED MATERIALS

Cover Photo: Shutterstock Images
Interior Photos: Shutterstock Images, 1, 5 (top), 5 (bottom left), 5 (bottom right), 7, 8, 9, 10–11, 12, 13, 16, 21; iStockphoto, 15, 19 (top), 19 (bottom left), 19 (bottom right), 20

Editor: Nick Rebman
Series Designer: Sophie Geister-Jones

Library of Congress Control Number: 2019942406

Publisher's Cataloging-in-Publication Data
Names: Vanden Branden, Claire, author.
Title: Swimming / by Claire Vanden Branden
Description: Minneapolis, Minnesota : Pop!, 2020 | Series: Kids' sports | Includes online resources and index.
Identifiers: ISBN 9781532165511 (lib. bdg.) | ISBN 9781532166839 (ebook)
Subjects: LCSH: Swimming--Juvenile literature. | Swimming for children--Juvenile literature. | Sports--Juvenile literature. | Sports for children--Juvenile literature.
Classification: DDC 797.2--dc23

Hello! My name is
Cody Koala

Pop open this book and you'll find QR codes like this one, loaded with information, so you can learn even more!

Scan this code* and others like it while you read, or visit the website below to make this book pop.

popbooksonline.com/swimming

*Scanning QR codes requires a web-enabled smart device with a QR code reader app and a camera.

Table of Contents

Chapter 1
Into the Water. 4

Chapter 2
Swimming Strokes 6

Chapter 3
Equipment. 14

Chapter 4
Swimming Safety. 18

Making Connections 22
Glossary. 23
Index 24
Online Resources 24

Chapter 1

Into the Water

A swimmer stands on a **starting block**. Then he dives into a pool. His arms move forward in circles. His legs kick hard. He is swimming.

starting block

Watch a video here!

5

Chapter 2

Swimming Strokes

There are four kinds of strokes in swimming. They are freestyle, butterfly, backstroke, and breaststroke.

Learn more here!

For freestyle, the legs do a **flutter kick**. The arms **alternate**.

For butterfly, the body moves like a wave. The legs do a **dolphin kick**. The arms go up and above the head.

For backstroke, swimmers stay on their backs. The arms move one at a time. Each arm goes up and out of the

water. Swimmers use the flutter kick.

> For backstroke, swimmers do not begin on top of the **starting blocks**. Instead, they begin in the water.

For breaststroke, a swimmer's arms move in a triangle shape underwater. The legs kick like a frog.

Swimming Strokes

Freestyle

Butterfly

Backstroke

Breaststroke

Chapter 3

Equipment

Swimmers **compete** in pools. Each swimmer stays in a **lane**. Swimming the length of the pool is one lap.

In the Olympics, one swimming race is 1,500 meters long. That is nearly one mile!

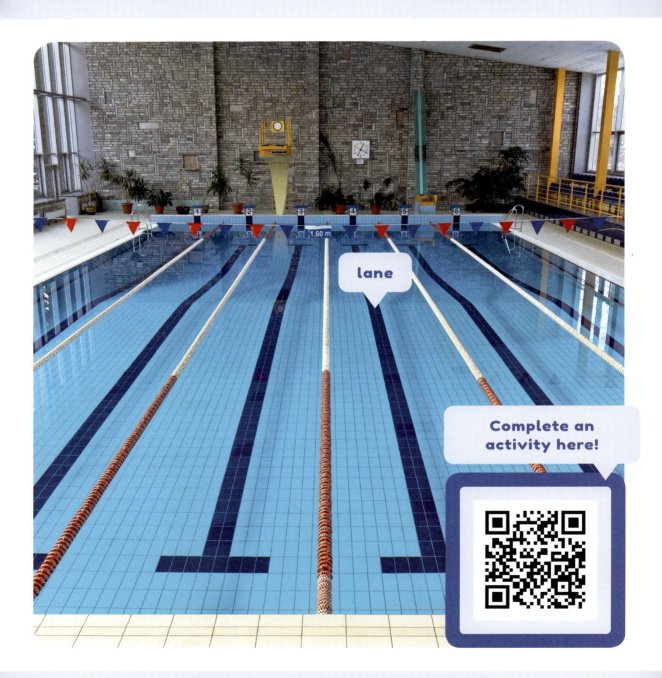

A swimmer needs to wear a swimsuit. A swimmer also needs to wear a swim cap and goggles. Swim caps cover the hair. Goggles help swimmers see underwater.

Chapter 4

Swimming Safety

Before swimmers start racing, they must take lessons. They learn how to do the strokes. They also learn how to stay safe in the water.

Learn more here!

19

Lifeguards help people stay safe too. They watch the pool. They jump into

the water if a swimmer is in trouble. They pull the swimmer to safety.

Making Connections

Text-to-Self

If you were going to swim in a race, which stroke would you use? Why?

Text-to-Text

Have you read books about other sports? How are those sports similar to swimming? How are they different?

Text-to-World

Swimmers need to follow rules to stay safe. Why do you think it is important to follow rules?

Glossary

alternate – to move one after the other.

compete – to take part in a game or race.

dolphin kick – a leg movement that is similar to how a dolphin moves its tail.

flutter kick – a leg movement where the feet switch off kicking hard.

lane – an area that is marked off for one person to swim in.

starting block – a platform that swimmers dive off of when they start a race.

Index

backstroke, 6, 10, 11, 13

breaststroke, 6, 12, 13

butterfly, 6, 9, 13

dolphin kick, 9

flutter kick, 8, 11

freestyle, 6, 8, 13

goggles, 16, 17

starting block, 4, 11

Online Resources

popbooksonline.com

Thanks for reading this Cody Koala book!

Scan this code* and others like it in this book, or visit the website below to make this book pop!

popbooksonline.com/swimming

*Scanning QR codes requires a web-enabled smart device with a QR code reader app and a camera.